LIFE IN A FROZEN WORLD

To the global community of Antarctic scientists and to the
schoolchildren around the world who are demanding that their
governments take action against climate change

—M. B.

To all researchers who work to better understand
the complexities of nature, especially in such a harsh environment as Antarctica.
And to my awesome wife Noni and our amazing daughter Nina, heartfelt thanks
for listening as I described all the wonders I discovered about
Antarctica during my research for the book

—T. G.

Published by
Peachtree Publishing Company Inc.
1700 Chattahoochee Avenue
Atlanta, Georgia 30318-2112
www.peachtree-online.com

Text © 2020 by Mary Batten
Illustrations © 2020 by Thomas Gonzalez

Edited by Vicky Holifield
Design and composition by Nicola Simmonds Carmack
and Adela Pons
Illustrations created in pastel, colored pencils,
and airbrush.

Printed in February by Toppan Leefung Ltd
10 9 8 7 6 5 4 3 2 1
First Edition
ISBN 978-1-68263-151-5

Cataloging-in-Publication Data is available from the
Library of Congress.

LIFE IN A FROZEN WORLD
Wildlife of Antarctica

Written by **Mary Batten**

Illustrated by **Thomas Gonzalez**

PEACHTREE
ATLANTA

Ice.
As far as the eye can see, blanketing
the continent on the bottom of the world.
Antarctica.
The coldest, windiest, driest place on Earth.

Yet in this extreme environment, life thrives.

Over millions of years, many living things—from microscopic bacteria to the blue whale, the largest animal that has ever lived—have evolved to survive on the ice, in the ice, and under the ice. Shaped by layers of snow and ice older than the human species, this frozen world is their home.

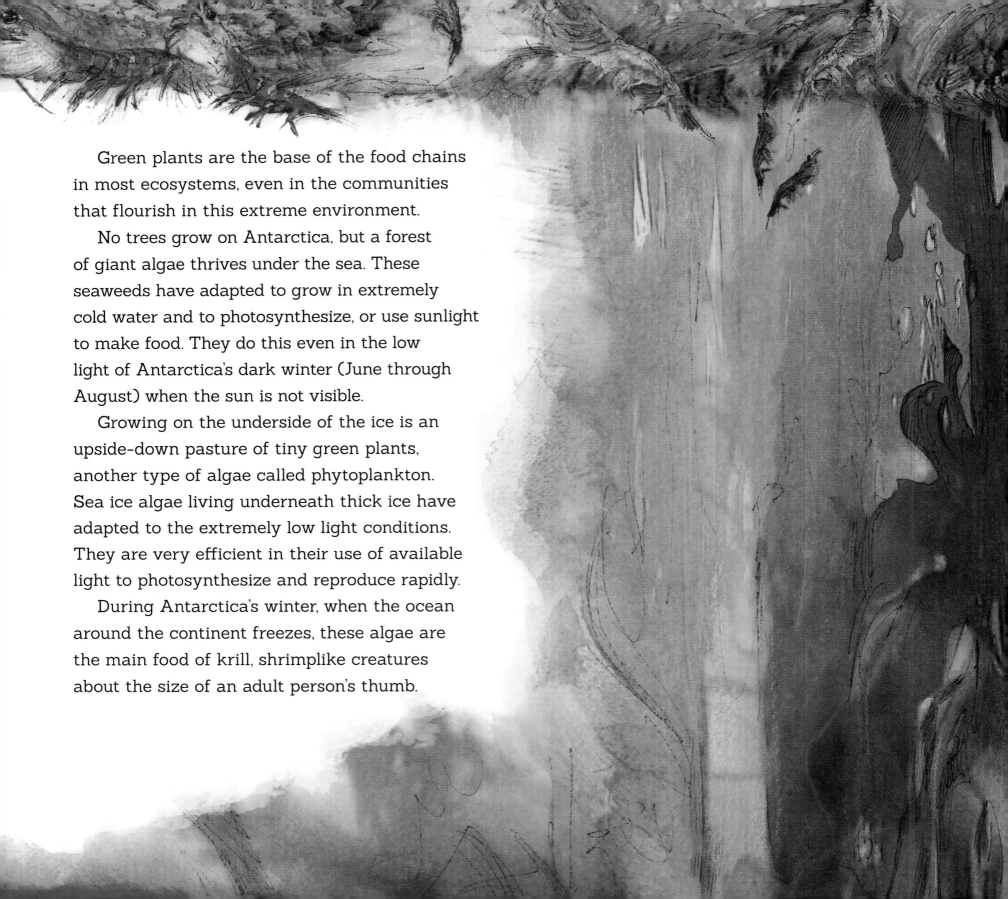

Green plants are the base of the food chains in most ecosystems, even in the communities that flourish in this extreme environment.

No trees grow on Antarctica, but a forest of giant algae thrives under the sea. These seaweeds have adapted to grow in extremely cold water and to photosynthesize, or use sunlight to make food. They do this even in the low light of Antarctica's dark winter (June through August) when the sun is not visible.

Growing on the underside of the ice is an upside-down pasture of tiny green plants, another type of algae called phytoplankton. Sea ice algae living underneath thick ice have adapted to the extremely low light conditions. They are very efficient in their use of available light to photosynthesize and reproduce rapidly.

During Antarctica's winter, when the ocean around the continent freezes, these algae are the main food of krill, shrimplike creatures about the size of an adult person's thumb.

Swimming in swarms so massive they can be seen from space, krill are the most abundant creatures in the Southern Ocean. They are called a "keystone species" because they play a key role in Antarctica's food chains. Krill have the amazing ability to shrink themselves and undergo long periods without food. These adaptations help them live through the severe cold of the Antarctic winter.

In the Southern Ocean, the species called Antarctic krill makes up an estimated biomass of over 500 million tons, roughly twice that of humans. Fish, seabirds, penguins, seals, whales, and other ocean creatures eat tons and tons of krill and many of them depend on this food source for survival.

Krill are a favorite food of icefish, the most unusual fish in the world. Sometimes they are called white-blooded fish because their blood is nearly as clear as water and their gills are white.

Icefish are the only vertebrates (animals with backbones) that do not make red blood cells. Humans and all other vertebrates make hemoglobin, the substance that makes blood red and carries oxygen to every cell in a creature's body. Icefish need oxygen, too, but they get it directly from the water instead of from red blood cells. They do not have scales like many other fish, so they are able to absorb the oxygen in the water directly through their skin and gills.

Icefish, like all other Antarctic fishes, have another remarkable adaptation that enables them to survive in frigid water: They produce a natural antifreeze protein that keeps their blood from freezing solid.

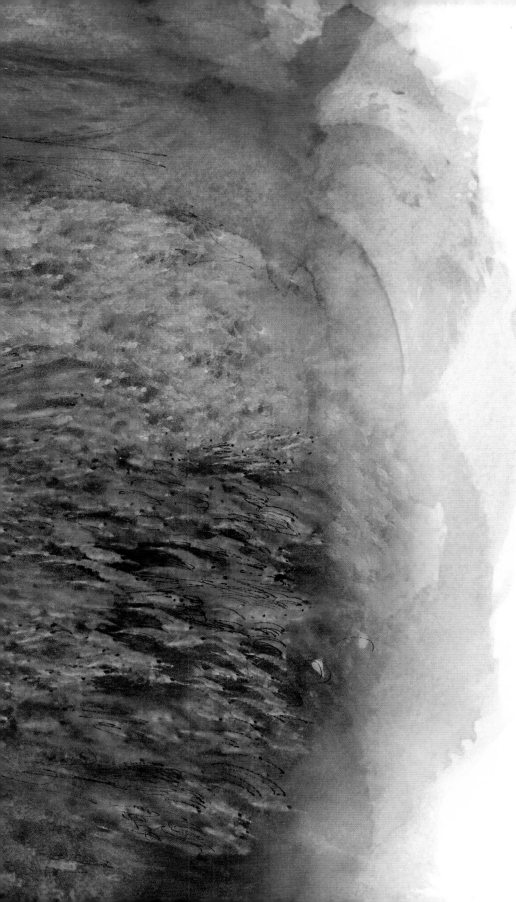

Many types of whales spend at least part of their lives in the icy waters around Antarctica.

They can live in this extreme environment for several reasons. They migrate to other regions during the coldest seasons. As warm-blooded mammals, they can increase their rate of burning calories and help stabilize the temperatures of their bodies in freezing conditions. And they have a dense layer of insulated fat called blubber under their skin to help them keep warm.

Humpback, minke, fin, blue, and other baleen whales feast on the plentiful krill in this extreme environment. When feeding, a baleen whale opens its gigantic mouth and takes a great gulp of water along with whatever small animals are swimming in it. Instead of teeth, these whales have baleen (long, thin plates hanging in rows from their upper jaws). When the whale pushes the water back out of its mouth, the baleen acts as a strainer, trapping food such as krill inside its mouth. A blue whale can eat four tons of krill a day.

Orcas, or killer whales, also live in Antarctic waters. Unlike baleen whales, they have teeth and eat not only krill, but also other animals such as seals and penguins.

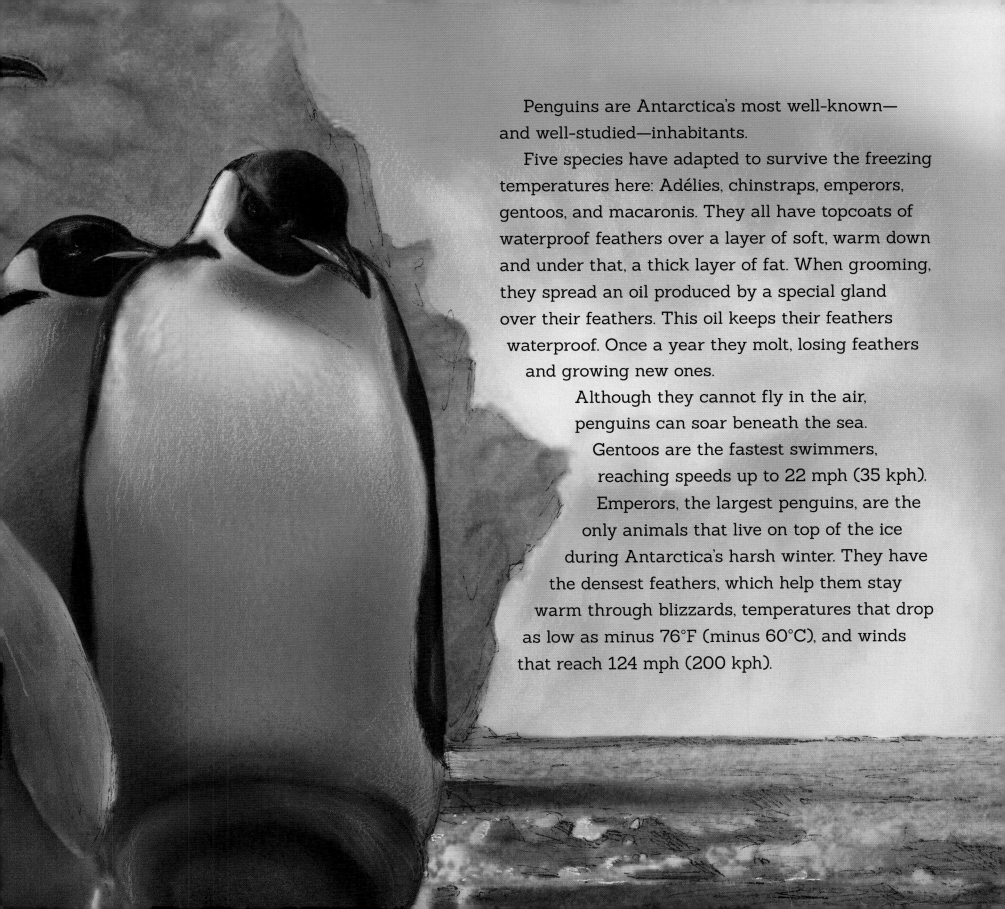

Penguins are Antarctica's most well-known—
and well-studied—inhabitants.

Five species have adapted to survive the freezing
temperatures here: Adélies, chinstraps, emperors,
gentoos, and macaronis. They all have topcoats of
waterproof feathers over a layer of soft, warm down
and under that, a thick layer of fat. When grooming,
they spread an oil produced by a special gland
over their feathers. This oil keeps their feathers
waterproof. Once a year they molt, losing feathers
and growing new ones.

Although they cannot fly in the air,
penguins can soar beneath the sea.
Gentoos are the fastest swimmers,
reaching speeds up to 22 mph (35 kph).
Emperors, the largest penguins, are the
only animals that live on top of the ice
during Antarctica's harsh winter. They have
the densest feathers, which help them stay
warm through blizzards, temperatures that drop
as low as minus 76°F (minus 60°C), and winds
that reach 124 mph (200 kph).

Fur seals, leopard seals, Ross seals, Weddell seals, crabeater seals, and elephant seals all give birth and care for their young on the ice. Thick layers of blubber insulate them against the cold.

During Antarctica's winter, Weddell seals live under the ice, where it is warmer than above. Their sharp, pointy front teeth are specially adapted for breaking through the ice to make breathing holes. When a female is ready to give birth, she uses her teeth to make a hole large enough to haul her heavy body up onto the ice to have her baby.

Crabeaters are the most abundant seals in Antarctica and the rest of the world. Despite their common name, they do not eat crabs. One crabeater seal can eat 30 pounds (14 kilograms) of krill a day. Little points on their teeth strain krill from the water. Crabeaters may make a hundred dives a day and spend eight to ten hours a day feeding. But they must constantly watch out for orcas and leopard seals hunting nearby.

Beneath the sea lies a hidden world teeming
with invertebrates (animals without backbones)—
soft corals, sponges, clams, gigantic worms, sea
squirts, sea stars, and many others. Sea stars,
or starfish, are the top predator in this world; they
feed primarily on other sea animals. Tiny shrimplike
creatures called amphipods graze on seaweed.

In these icy waters, creatures grow more slowly and live
longer than in temperate seas. Sea urchins and scallops may
live a century. Antarctic sponges are the longest-lived animals
on the planet.

Some Antarctic creatures grow to giant size. Sea spiders as large
as a dinner plate don't have gills or lungs but absorb oxygen through
their skin. Their spindly legs hold their guts, which not only digest
their food but also pump blood. Nobody knows why some creatures
grow so huge in polar waters. It may be related to the fact that
cold water holds more oxygen than warmer water.

Antarctica has no native human population. People never adapted to living year-round in this frozen wilderness. It is the most pristine environment on Earth, the home to many complex and delicately balanced ecosystems. But humans have found ways to explore much of the continent and to carry on science there.

Antarctica is the only continent protected for peace and science. Fifty-four countries have signed the 1959 Antarctic Treaty, preserving the continent for scientific investigation and "peaceful purposes only." Thirty nations have research stations on the continent. Scientists working there share information and work together in the true spirit of cooperation and peace.

Over millions of years, Antarctica's creatures have evolved to thrive in their icy habitats, and they have lived in balance with each other and their extreme environment. But will they be able to adapt to changes that are now happening at a much faster rate than in past centuries? Can they survive in a warmer world?

The atmosphere and ocean are warming around the western Antarctica Peninsula at an increasing pace. The ice is melting, and the resulting changes affect every living organism on the continent. Specialists in many scientific fields are leading expeditions to Antarctica to learn more about the impact of climate change.

During Antarctica's short summer—from November through February, when the sun shines most of the time—scientists arrive from all over the world. While the weather is milder, researchers carry out a wide variety of studies—from examining changes in snowfall patterns to measuring the growth of under-the-ice algae.

One method used by scientists to learn about the changing conditions in this part of the world is collecting ice cores from the ice sheet covering the continent. Ice cores hold thousands of years of Antarctica's climate history frozen in time and show how its past climate compares with today's. Like tree rings, bands of white and varying shades of gray on an ice core teach scientists about conditions over time. Bubbles in the ice tell scientists how much carbon dioxide—the greenhouse gas warming the planet—was in the air at a certain point in time. The oldest continuous core record, taken from bedrock almost two miles below the ice, is 800,000 years old.

A lot of the scientific work in Antarctica is done underwater where most of the continent's animals and plants live. Scuba-diving scientists are studying how changes in the sea ice affect animal communities in Antarctica's shallow coastal waters.

Young krill usually spend the Antarctic winter fattening up on the algae that grows under the ice. But the amount of sea ice is shrinking, and the large species of algae that the young krill prefer has been replaced by a smaller species. As a result, fewer young krill make it to adulthood, and their population is decreasing.

Scientists also worry that icefish might not be able to survive the warming of Antarctica's waters. For the last 10 to 14 million years, the water temperature of the Southern Ocean has been below 41°F (5°C). Many of these fish might die if the temperature rises only a few more degrees.

Every November for at least the last 700 years, thousands of Adélie penguins have come to Torgersen Island along the northwestern coast of Antarctica to breed, lay their eggs, and raise their young. But both sea and air temperatures in this area are warming faster than other parts of Antarctica. As a result, humidity has risen, causing unseasonable snowstorms.

Now it snows while female penguins are incubating their eggs. When the snow melts, the melt water drowns the eggs, wiping out the next generation of penguins. There were once 15,000 breeding pairs, but there are now fewer than 3,000.

As the pack ice melts, the Adélies must also swim farther and farther to find enough krill to eat. They may one day disappear from the Antarctic Peninsula.

Floating ice shelves thousands of feet thick form a kind of dam around Antarctica, keeping the towering land-based glaciers (huge, slowly moving masses of accumulated ice) from flowing into the sea. But the sea temperatures are rising, and the ice shelves are melting. Scientists who have worked for many years at the U.S. Palmer Station on Anvers Island now hear daily the thunderous roar of calving—the breaking away of enormous chunks of ice—from a nearby glacier.

The loss of sea ice is endangering the habitat of krill, and the alarming drop in the krill population means a greatly reduced food source for other sea creatures. The decline in sea ice is also a threat to species that depend on it as a place to reproduce.

Antarctica may seem too far away to affect us, but rising temperatures of atmosphere and ocean in this frozen world not only affects the species that make their homes here, they also affect the weather and climate in other parts of our planet.

Scientists estimate that the melting of Antarctica's land ice will lead to a rise in sea level of between 3 and 16 inches (.8 and 41 centimeters) by 2100.

Antarctica is telling us we must take action to keep this frozen world that has existed for millions of years from melting into the sea over the next few centuries.

Antarctica's creatures depend on the ice.

In the long term, so do we.

ANTARCTICA

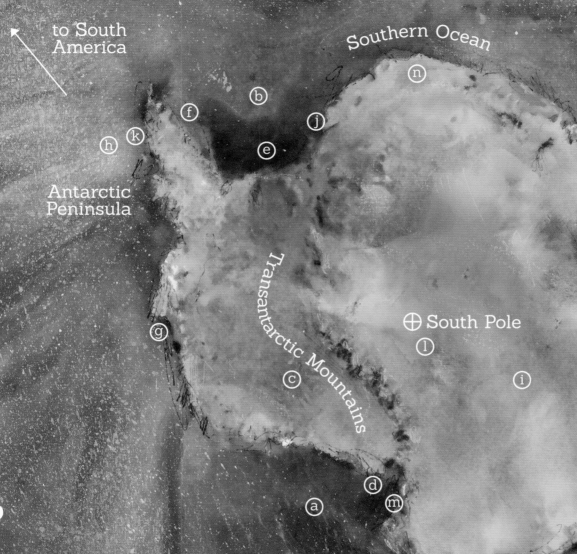

to South
America

Southern Ocean

ⓝ

ⓑ

ⓕ

ⓙ

ⓚ

ⓗ

ⓔ

Antarctic
Peninsula

Transantarctic Mountains

⊕ South Pole

ⓛ

ⓖ

ⓘ

ⓒ

ⓓ

ⓐ

ⓜ

Southern Ocean

LEGEND

ⓐ Ross Sea

ⓑ Weddell Sea

ⓒ Mt. Vinson

ⓓ Ross Ice Shelf

ⓔ Ronne Ice Shelf

ⓕ Larsen Ice Shelf

ⓖ Thwaites Glacier

ⓗ Torgersen Island

ⓘ Russian research station at Vostok

ⓙ UK research station at Halley

ⓚ US research station at Palmer Station

ⓛ US research station at Amundsen-Scott South Pole

ⓜ US research station at McMurdo

ⓝ Norwegian research station at Troll

There are 76 research stations in Antarctica. Forty are permanent, operating year-round, and 36 are seasonal, operating during Antarctica's summer. This map shows only a few of them.

LEARN MORE ABOUT ANTARCTICA

1 The circumpolar current that flows clockwise around Antarctica is the largest current on Earth. It affects climate around the world.

2 The Southern Ocean is the only one that connects with every other ocean on Earth.

3 The lowest temperature ever recorded on Earth, minus 128.6°F (minus 89.2°C), was measured at Russia's Antarctic Vostok Station on July 21, 1983.

4 During the 1930s, Norwegian Ingrid Christensen was the first woman to set foot on the Antarctic continent. As part of her husband's expeditions, she made four trips there. Since then many women scientists have worked in Antarctica.

5 Mount Vinson, at 16,050 feet (4,892 meters), is the highest peak in Antarctica.

6 NASA has discovered that about 14 billion tons of ice from under the Thwaites Glacier in West Antarctica has melted. This cavity is two-thirds the size of Manhattan Island in New York.

7 Norwegian explorer Roald Amundsen, the first person to reach the South Pole, planted his country's flag there on December 14, 1911.

8 On a sealing expedition in 1820, Nathaniel B. Palmer, for whom Palmer Station is named, was the first American to sight Antarctica.

9 The Ross Ice Shelf, the size of France, is the largest floating body of ice in the world.

10 In 1823, British explorer and whaling captain James Weddell discovered the sea and the seal that are named after him.

"A meter of sea-level rise comes from only two-percent change in the Antarctic ice sheet, and a meter of sea-level rise displaces a hundred million people around the planet."

—Gary Wilson, Professor of Marine Science
Otago University, New Zealand

"The estimated total biomass of Antarctic krill exceeds that of the weight of the Earth's eight billion–plus human population!"

—Maggie Amsler, Researcher
University of Alabama at Birmingham

Author's Note

My fascination with Antarctica began years ago when I was working for The Cousteau Society, which was conducting a campaign to save Antarctica from mineral exploitation and protect it for future generations. To dramatize the campaign, famed ocean explorer Jacques Cousteau took six children, one from each continent, to Antarctica, and we collected tens of thousands of signatures on petitions from schoolchildren in many countries. Twenty-nine years later, in 2019, schoolchildren from approximately one hundred countries marched in the streets to urge their governments to take action against climate change. "Act as if the house is on fire, because it is," said sixteen-year-old Swedish student Greta Thunberg, who had sparked the student movement a year earlier when she sat in front of the Swedish parliament protesting her country's lack of action on climate change.

"Climate change in Antarctica is not just an issue for life in Antarctica but for all of us on the planet. Antarctica influences weather and climate in both the Atlantic and Pacific of the northern hemispehere.."

—James B McClintock,
Endowed University Professor of Polar & Marine Biology
University of Alabama at Birmingham

Today's young people are rightly concerned. What adults do, or don't do, today will affect their world tomorrow. They know what climate science is telling us. They know that they will inherit the problems of a rapidly warming planet.

Although some world leaders falsely claim climate change is a hoax and refuse to accept the findings of science, the evidence from thousands of studies and record-breaking weather events continues to pile up. Climate change is not just a bunch of statistics in a scientific report. It is not only affecting Antarctica's creatures, it is affecting people's lives everywhere.

The fact that Antarctica, a world that has been frozen for millions of years, is warming in our lifetime should ring alarm bells about the seriousness of climate change for our entire planet. No place on Earth, not even this frozen continent on the bottom of the world, is exempt from the effects of climate change.

The hopeful news is that when we know what causes a problem, we have the means to look for ways to solve it. But once we find solutions, we have to act. All of us must make a commitment to protect Antarctica and the entire Earth for present and future generations by drastically reducing the use of fossil fuels and speeding up the development of alternate energy sources such as wind and solar.

This quote from a researcher who has spent his career studying wildlife in Antarctica sends us a clear message concerning the climate change crisis there and in the rest of the world:

"No one country is going to solve it on its own. It's going to take each and every one of us to make a difference."

—Gary Wilson,
Professor of Marine Science
Otago University, New Zealand

Glossary

algae
a diverse group of plantlike organisms, many of which grow in or near water and have the ability to conduct photosynthesis

biomass
the amount of living matter in a habitat

calving
the breaking off of ice from the edge of a glacier, forming icebergs

climate
the average condition of the weather in a particular place over a long period of time

ecosystem
a community of plants and animals living in balance with each other and with their environment

food chain
an arrangement of organisms in an ecosystem in which each group feeds on the one below it

hemoglobin
protein in red blood cells that gives them their red color; hemoglobin transports oxygen to all the tissues of vertebrates

ice core
a long cylinder of ice obtained by drilling into an ice sheet

phytoplankton
tiny plants, also called microalgae, found in oceans, streams, and lakes

weather
the state of the atmosphere, with respect to heat, cold, humidity, storms, cloudiness, dryness, etc., in a particular time and place

swimming sea snail
(*Limacina rangii*)

Acknowledgments

Writing this book has been a labor of love and discovery. Most rewarding has been reaching out to scientists doing the real fieldwork that advances our knowledge of Antarctica. I am profoundly grateful to the following who generously shared their work with me and answered my questions by phone and/or email: Maggie Amsler, Researcher, University of Alabama at Birmingham; Kamil Murat Aydin, Associate Researcher, Department of Earth System Science, University of California, Irvine; H. William Detrich, III, Ph.D., Professor of Biochemistry and Marine Biology, Northeastern University College of Science, Boston, Mass.; Nick Golledge, Associate Professor, Antarctic Research Centre, Victoria University of Wellington, New Zealand; Sabrina Heiser, Ph.D. Candidate, University of Alabama at Birmingham; James B. McClintock, Endowed University Professor of Polar and Marine Biology, University of Alabama at Birmingham; Gary Wilson, Professor of Marine Science, Otago University, New Zealand.

Publishing a book like this requires a team of skilled people and I feel extremely fortunate to have such a brilliant team at Peachtree. Profound thanks to Margaret Quinlin, President and Publisher, for believing in my work. I thank illustrator Tom Gonzalez for creating the stunning images that bring the words to life; Nicki Carmack and Adela Pons for the book's attractive design and layout. Huge thanks to wonderful, super editor Vicky Holifield, with whom I have had the privilege of working on four previous books. Her insightful comments and wise critique always push my creativity and help to make each book the best it can be. Finally I thank my agent Barbara Markowitz and Harvey Markowitz for their long-time support and friendship.

Selected Bibliography

Books

McClintock, James. *Lost Antarctica*. Palgrave/Macmillan, New York: 2012.

Montaigne, Fen. *Fraser's Penguins: A Journey to the Future in Antarctica*. Henry Holt and Company, New York: 2010.

Pollack, Henry, Ph.D. *A World Without Ice*. Foreword by Al Gore. Avery, New York: 2009.

Thomas, Keltie. *Rising Seas: Flooding, Climate Change and Our New World*. Firefly Books Ltd, Ontario: 2018.

Walker, Gabrielle. *Antarctica: An Intimate Portrait of a Mysterious Continent*. Houghton Mifflin Harcourt, Boston: 2013.

Websites

Australia Antarctic Division *www.antarctica.gov.au*

Antarctica New Zealand *www.antarcticanz.govt.nz/about-us/partnerships*

Intergovernmental Panel on Climate Change (IPCC) *www.ipcc.ch*

National Oceanic and Atmospheric Administration *www.noaa.gov/climate*

Palmer Station Webcams *www.usap.gov/videoclipsandmaps/palwebcam.cfm*

United States Antarctic Program *www.usap.gov*

Videos & Films

Antarctic Krill - *Euphausia superba*, Cool Antarctica *www.coolantarctica.com/Antarctica%20fact%20file/wildlife/krill.php*

Antarctica is a Barometer of Global Change. Dr. Jim McClintock TED talk *www.youtube.com/watch?v=meHunVXB-3c*

Don't Ever Let Anyone Tell You that there are no Forests in Antarctica, written by Chuck Amsler, April 12, 2018. *www.uab.edu/antarctica/expeditions/2018/forests-of-antarctica*

Invertebrates at Palmer Station *www.youtube.com/watch?v=fW_xeEJHUTY*

Ice Core Drilling at the South Pole *www.youtube.com/watch?v=h9p1sWhYFqE*

McMurdo Oceanographic Observatory Watch live underwater video streamed from Antarctica *www.moo-antarctica.net/about*

National Science Foundation Ice Core Storage Facility *www.icecores.org/about-ice-cores*

Shackleton's Voyage of Endurance (NOVA) 2002 *www.youtube.com/watch?v=XxkOpJRevj0*

University of Alabama at Birmingham in Antarctica *www.uab.edu/antarctica*